A Good Heart

Written by Linda Rieger
Illustrations by John Bianchi

Text © Pathways Into Science® Inc. 2007
Illustrations © Adobe Artworks Inc. 2007
ISBN 0-9779427-4-0

www.pathwaysintoscience.net

This web site takes you to all of the Internet links described on page 16.

Go to: **See Books**
Use the password: **heart7**

Visit the linked sites with your children. The sites were chosen because they are engaging and appropriate for young children. Pathways into Science® cannot be responsible for any virus that might possibly be downloaded when visiting them.

All rights reserved.
No part of this publication may be reproduced or transmitted in any form or by any means, electronic or mechanical, including photocopy, recording, taping or any existing or future information storage and retrieval system, without permission in writing from the author and the illustrator.

"Grandpa, how come you are still so strong?
How can you stay healthy living this long?"

"Because I have a good heart inside."
"A good heart?" I said as we walked outside.

"I walk everyday most of the time. Always using a car is not so fine. So .... I have a good heart!"

"Walking in the woods is the best solution.
I stay away from noise and air pollution.
So .... I have a good heart!"

"Drinking clean water is another tip.
I do my part to have good water to sip.
So ...... I have a good heart!"

"Eating good food with very small bites,
Keep fats, sugars, and salt low….that's right!
So …..I have a good heart!"

"Sharing with others all around,
And being happy helps, I've found.
So.... I have a good heart."

"I do not smoke, sniff, or take bad drugs.
I get all my highs from great big hugs.
So...I have a good heart."

"Seeing a good doctor to check me out,
Staying healthy is what it's all about.
So... I have a good heart!"

"There is another part that is hard to see. Having friends and staying calm are good for me.
So.... I have a good heart."

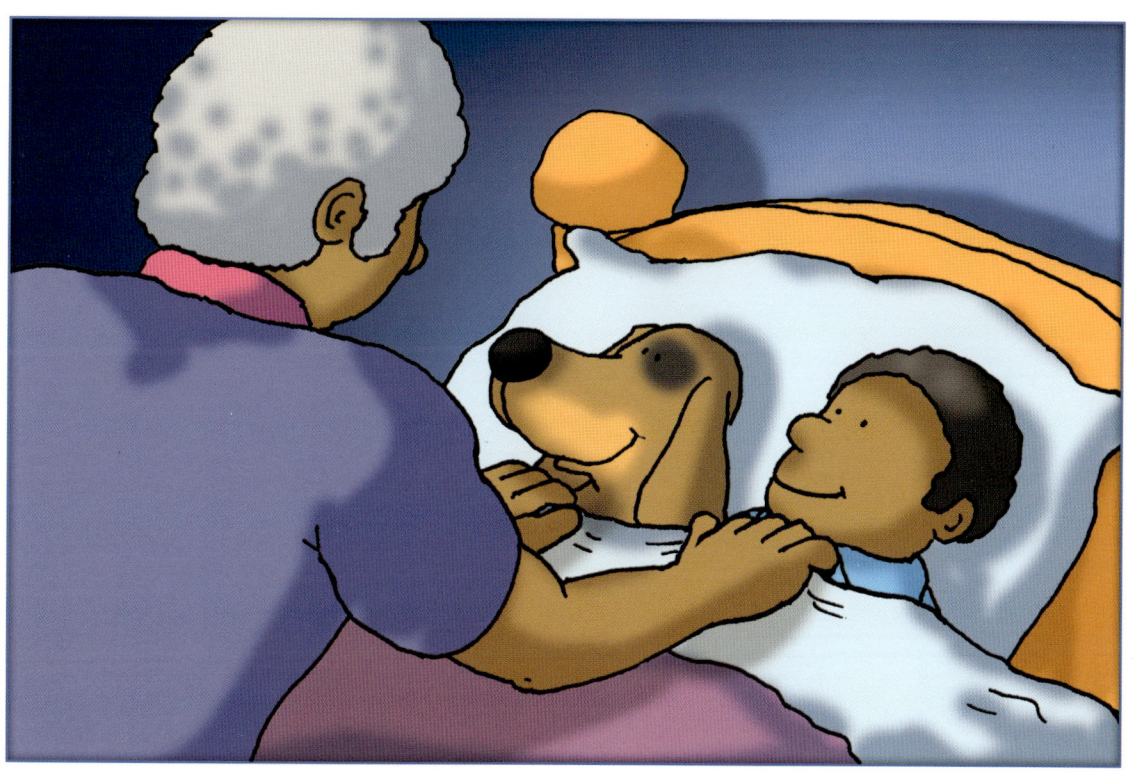

"Thank you, Grandpa, for all of your advice.
I know that doing those things will all be nice."

"I want all of my friends to have a good heart.

Telling them how, will be my part."

Being a calm person is good for your body's heart. People who share with their friends and family usually live longer than people who are alone, angry, or unhappy.

Most people know that you have to eat good food like whole grains, fruits, and vegetables in small amounts to have a healthy heart. Good food builds strong muscles. People with muscles live longer than people who have lots of fat. But surprise, scientists now know that too much noise or bad smells — like from spray cans or markers — can also hurt your heart.

Clean air, clean water, sleep, and exercise are all a part of having a healthy body and heart. To make sure you stay well, trips to the doctor and dentist for check ups are important. It is also important for you to check out how to keep the earth's air and water healthy. Tell others what you know.

Keep strong. Exercise the most important muscle of them all....your heart!

Go to **www.pathwaysintoscience.net** and find this book. Use password: **Heart7**

Click on **Web site 1** to see funny videos about good food and exercise. Try the games, songs and videos on the other websites.

Find out why smoking is bad for your heart.

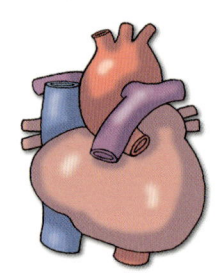